MARINA SEVESO

The Antique & Flea Markets of ITALY

D0311464

translated by
Oonagh Stransky

THE LITTLE BOOKROOM
NEW YORK

EDITOR'S NOTE

We have left the names of towns and cities
in Italian. Phone numbers, denoted by the
telephone icon, are for a variety of town halls,
tourism offices, or Chambers of Commerce,
that have information about the flea markets.

The Little Bookroom
1755 Broadway, 5th floor
New York NY 10019
(212) 293-1643 F (212) 333-5374
editorial@littlebookroom.com

Location Listings

Vigevano (Pv)

VENETO
Adria (Ro)
Asolo (Tv)
Belluno
Cadoneghe (Pd)
Este (Pd)
Gallio (Vi)
Jesolo (Ve)
Marostica (Vi)
Montegrotto (Pd)
Noale (Ve)
Noventa di Piave (Ve)
Noventa Vicentina (Vi)
Padova
Piazzola sul Brenta (Pd)
Pieve di Cadore (Bl)
Recoaro Terme (Vi)
Soave (Vr)
Treviso
Verona
Villafranca di Verona
  (Vr)

**FRIULI-VENEZIA
GIULIA**
Gorizia
Trieste
Udine

EMILIA ROMAGNA
Bagnacavallo (Ra)
Bologna
Cervia (Ra)
Cesena
Cortemaggiore (Pc)

Faenza (Ra)
Ferrara
Fiorenzuola d'Arda (Pc)
Fontanellato (Pr)
Gualtieri (Re)
Imola (Bo)
Lugo (Ra)
Mirandola (Mo)
Modena
Novellara (Re)
Piacenza
Ravenna
San Secondo (Pr)
Santarcangelo di
  Romagna (Rn)
Sant'Ilario d'Enza (Re)

TOSCANA
Anghiari (Ar)
Arezzo
Firenze
Lucca
Montepulciano (Si)
Orbetello (Gr)
Pietrasanta (Lu)
Pisa
Pistoia
San Miniato (Pi)
Siena
Vinci (Fi)

MARCHE
Acquaviva Picena (Ap)
Ancona
Ascoli Piceno
Civitanova Marche (Mc)
Fano (Pu)

Fermo (Ap)
Gradara (Pu)
Grottammare (Ap)
Matelica (Mc)
Pesaro
Porto Recanati (Mc)
Recanati (Mc)
San Benedetto del
Tronto (Ap)
Senigallia (An)
Tolentino (Mc)

UMBRIA
Città di Castello (Pg)
Narni (Tr)
Passignano sul
Trasimeno (Pg)
Perugia
Pissignano di Campello
  (Pg)
Spoleto (Pg)

LAZIO
Albano Laziale (Rm)
Anagni (Fr)
Bracciano (Rm)
Campagnano (Rm)
Frosinone
Latina
Monterotondo (Rm)
Rieti
Roma
Veroli (Fr)
Viterbo

ABRUZZO
Avezzano (Aq)

Chieti
L'Aquila
Lanciano (Ch)

CAMPANIA
Napoli
Salerno
San Lorenzello (Bn)

PUGLIA
Bari
Brindisi
Lecce
Ostuni (Br)
Rutigliano (Ba)
Squinziano (Le)
Taranto

BASILICATA
Matera

CALABRIA
Crotone
Palmi (Rc)
Reggio Calabria
Rossano (Cs)

SICILY
Catania
Mascalucia (Ct)

SARDEGNA
Cagliari
Sassari

The First Saturday & Sunday of the Month

AREZZO

The Antique Fair that takes place in Piazza San Francesco and Piazza Grande is one of the most important antique markets: more than a thousand vendors come from all regions of Italy and parts of Europe. The variety of merchandise for sale is vast, including collectibles, ethnic artifacts and the work of local craftsmen.

☎ 057523952

GENOVA

Roughly seventy-five stands are set up in the atrium of the Ducal Palace for this event. Its specialties include furniture, ex-voto work, period jewelry, clothing and silver. Furnishings from the Forties and Fifties are also popular.

☎ 010576791

ORBETELLO (GROSSETO)

Approximately fifty stands fill the historic center.

☎ 0564850133

RECANATI (MACERATA)

The one hundred stands on display in Piazza Leopardi offer items such as furniture, furnishings, jewelry, tapestries, books and antique fabrics.

☎ 0719799084

REGGIO CALABRIA

Close to fifty vendors set up their wares at the Town Lido.

☎ 096521171

SPOLETO (PERUGIA)

MERCATO DELLE BRICIOLE
(MARKET OF CRUMBS)

In Piazza del Mercato and along the narrow streets of the town center, more than fifty stands display a wide selection of products, especially handicrafts, antiques and collectibles.

☎ 074349890

The First Saturday of the Month

CESENA
Seventy merchants set up shop in the historic center of town.
☎ 047356111

COMO
In the picturesque Piazza San Fedele a small number of vendors (around twenty) show their wares in what has become a tradition for this city.
☎ 031950204

ROMANO DI LOMBARDIA (BERGAMO)
Seventy vendors line up under the porticoes in the historic center of town.
☎ 0363913928

SAVONA
In Piazza Chabrol and along via Paleocapa nearly a hundred stands offer minor collectibles, from prints to postcards.
☎ 0198402321

The First Sunday of the Month

BRINDISI
Fifty stands fill Piazza Santa Teresa for this event.
☎ 0831562126

CASTIGLIONE OLONA (VARESE)
FIERA DEL CARDINALE
(THE CARDINAL'S FAIR)
Fifty tables, consisting principally of gift items, are set up in Piazza Castiglioni.
☎ 0331691848

CORTEMAGGIORE (PIACENZA)
ANTIQUARIATO E COSE D'ALTRI TEMPI
(THINGS FROM DAYS OF YORE)
In Piazza Patrioti and along via Roma, under the porticoes of the historic town center, about two hundred stands offer a wide selection of goods.
☎ 0523832172

COSTA MEZZATE (BERGAMO)
ANTIQUARIATO IN CASCINA
(ANTIQUES IN THE PARK)
Close to eighty vendors attend this picturesque fair, which is held in the Cascina Fui park. Every month, except August.
☎ 035217257

CROTONE

One hundred vendors set up their stands in Piazza Duomo. Worth noting is the selection of collector's pipes, old wooden utensils and jewelry.

☎ 09627636

DESENZANO DEL GARDA (BRESCIA)

Every month (except January and August), seventy merchants set up in Piazza Malvezzi, offering a vast selection of English silver, walking sticks, jewelry, china and glass.

☎ 03045052

FERRARA

In Piazza Municipio and Piazza Savonarola approximately fifty stands offer everything from antique giftware to simply old objects. This market is held every month, excluding August.

☎ 800225830 (toll free)

FROSINONE

Every month, except July and August, more than one hundred vendors from all over Italy set up their wares in Piazza Valchera and along via Angeloni.

☎ 800229394 (toll free)

GORIZIA

More than fifty participants set up their stands in Piazza Tommaseo, offering articles they've gathered from house to house, including old magazines, newspapers and bijoux.

☎ 0481383111

LA SPEZIA

Eighty vendors fill Piazza Cavour.

☎ 0187770900

LATINA

More than two hundred stands enliven the town square with antiques, old objects and handicrafts.

☎ 0773695407

MALGRATE (LECCO)

From May to November some sixty vendors gather on the lake's edge; from December to April they line the roads of the center of town. There is no market in August.

☎ 0341362360

MAROSTICA (VICENZA)

MERCATO D'ANTIQUARIATO
(ANTIQUE MARKET)

Piazza Castello, the same square where the famous game of chess with human pieces is played, is host to approximately one hundred and twenty dealers — there's an excellent choice of furniture at this market.

☎ 042472800

MATERA

Eighty stands fill Piazza Vittorio Veneto.

☎ 0835331983

MONCALIERI (TORINO)

RABADAN AN PIASSA
(RUMMAGE IN PIAZZA)

Furniture, china, lace and more — the word rabadan in Piemontese dialect means a jumble of objects. More than one hundred and fifty stands are set up in Piazza Vittorio Emanuele for this rendezvous.

☎ 011606188

NOVELLARA (REGGIO EMILIA)

This market takes place every month, except August, in the old part of town. About one hundred booths take part.

☎ 0522662718

NOVENTA VICENTINA (VICENZA)

MERCATINO DELL' USATO
(USED GOODS MARKET)

Some of the finds at this market, which takes place under the porticoes and in Piazza IV Novembre, include early modern objects, furniture and good deals.

☎ 0444544122

PAVIA

Old books, early radios sets, and early twentieth century furnishings are some of the specialties of this market, which is made up of nearly a hundred stands and takes place in Piazza della Vittoria.

☎ 038222156

PIETRASANTA (LUCCA)

Highlights of this market include furniture, marble, and wooden sculpture. It is held in Piazza Duomo, with the participation of nearly seventy merchants.

☎ 058391991

PISSIGNANO DI CAMPELLO (PERUGIA)

More than two hundred stands line via Flaminia Vecchia, offering minor antiques and furniture at interesting prices; paintings from the seventeenth and eighteenth century are also frequently found here.

☎ 075575951

ROMA

More than one hundred and seventy vendors gather near Ponte Milvio for this event.

☎ 06488991

RUTIGLIANO (BARI)

In the historic center of town, fifty dealers sell a wide array of goods, but this market is especially known for china, ceramics, metals, old handcrafted tools, as well as hand-sewn lingerie.

☎ 0804761108

SABBIONETA (MANTOVA)

Fifty stands specializing in giftware line via Gonzaga.

☎ 0376328253

SAINT-VINCENT (AOSTA)

Thirty merchants fill the town square.

☎ 016533352

SAN MINIATO (PISA)

Under the loggia of San Domenico, in addition to antiques and collectibles, this market has a good selection of furniture, both Italian and ethnic (Indian, mainly).

☎ 05042291

SANTARCANGELO DI ROMAGNA (RIMINI)

LA CASA DEL TEMPO
(THE HOUSE OF TIME)

Furniture, silver, china, musical instruments, as well as collectibles restored by local artisans are only some of the treasures available in Piazza Ganganelli. More than a hundred vendors are present for this event.

☎ 0541356111

SANTENA (TORINO)

MERCATINO DI PORTA PORTESE

In Piazza Martiri della Libertà and along the surrounding streets three hundred dealers buy, sell and trade wares. No market in August.

☎ 0119456509

SQUINZIANO (LECCE)

Furniture, coins, stamps and miniature models are on view in Piazza Vittoria.

☎ 0832314117

UDINE

Sixty vendors gather in Piazza Matteoti; no market in January or August.

☎ 0432295972

VERCELLI

L'BARLAFUS

The name of this market is local dialect for odds and ends. It takes place in Piazza Cavour, and more than sixty vendors take part. Despite its name, this market specializes in antiques of good quality.

☎ 0161252622

The Second Saturday & Sunday of the Month

ASOLO (TREVISO)

MERCATINO DELL'ANTIQUARIATO
(ANTIQUE MARKET)

This is one of the most prestigious antique markets in the region, and one of the most important in all of Italy. It takes place in Piazza del Mercato and is held from September to June. Fabric, jewelry, watches, furniture and collectibles are its specialties. The market opens on Saturday afternoon.

☎ 042355967

BRACCIANO (ROMA)

One hundred vendors gather in the historic center of town; objects from the Forties and Fifties are prevalent.

☎ 0648991

BRESCIA

Seventy vendors display their goods under the porticoes of Piazza della Vittoria. Antiques, African and Asian arts are favored.

☎ 03045052

CHIAVARI (GENOVA)

This is one of the most famous antique markets in Liguria; it takes place on via Martiri della Liberazione and in the small Piazzas around town. More than one hundred stands contribute to make it an exciting event. Local handicrafts — lace, macramé, linens — as well as the famous Chiavari chairs, are prevalent; there is also a good choice of prints and old advertisements that some dealers offer already framed and matted. Other kinds of graphic arts, foreign furnishings and collectibles are also available.

☎ 010530821

FANO (PESARO-URBINO)

In the historic center of town more than one hundred merchants offer period furnishings, including choice Art Deco and Liberty pieces.

☎ 072130462

L'AQUILA

Approximately eighty stands gather in Piazza Santa Maria Paganica and Piazza Chiarino.

☎ 0862410808

MASCALUCIA (CATANIA)

FIERA ANTIQUARIA DELL'ETNA (THE MT. ETNA ANTIQUE FAIR)

This market takes place in Piazza Falcone e Borsellino and consists of more than a hundred vendors. It is easily considered one of the most important antique markets in Sicily; merchants from all parts of Southern Italy attend the event. Antiques of all kinds are available, especially rustic Sicilian pieces.

☎ 800841042 (toll free)

MONTEPULCIANO (SIENA)

For this much adored and anticipated event, fifty merchants gather in the historic center of town.

☎ 0577226732

PISA

More than one hundred exhibitors lay out their goods under the loggias where the silk and wool market once stood, offering antiques of various kinds. Closed in July and August.

☎ 05042291

PISTOIA

This market takes place along via Pacinotti, in indoor locales, and is made up of a hundred and fifty stands. Collectibles and modern art pieces are only some of its specialties. Closed in July and August.

☎ 057334326

The Second Saturday of the Month

ADRIA (ROVIGO)

This antique and hobby market takes place along Braghin arcade and in Piazza Bocchi.

☎ 800221471 (toll free)

BOLOGNA

This market takes place in Piazza Santo Stefano in front of church of the same name — it specializes in LP records, Forties style furniture and oriental art. Approximately eighty-five vendors show their wares.

☎ 051204111

GROTTAMMARE (ASCOLI PICENO)

In the town center more than fifty vendors take part in this lively market, which features collectibles, artisanal work and modern pieces.

☎ 0736253045

PIADENA (CREMONA)

Held under the porticoes of the old town center, this characteristic flea market is made up of more than fifty merchants and their stands.

☎ 037223233

The Second Sunday of the Month

ALBANO LAZIALE (ROMA)

This market, which is affectionately known as "In the Footsteps of the Past," takes place near the baths of Cellomaio; close to one hundred and fifty vendors take part.

☎ 06421381

CARMAGNOLA (TORINO)

IL MERCÀ D'LE PÛLES (FLEA MARKET)

The historic center of town plays host to more than one hundred stands, offering minor antiques, collectibles, local crafts and farming tools.

☎ 0119724111

CASTELLONE (CREMONA)

More than two hundred vendors set up their wares under the porticoes; large items like cars and antique motorcycles are sometimes for sale. No market in August.

☎ 037223233

CASTELSEPRIO (VARESE)

Approximately one hundred and twenty vendors set up shop in the historic center of town.

☎ 0331820501

FIRENZE

ARTI E MESTIERI (ARTS AND CRAFTS)

This market takes place every month (except August) in Piazza Santo Spirito and is composed of seventy merchants' stands, which exhibit everything from antiques to local crafts.

☎ 05523320

GUALTIERI (REGGIO EMILIA)

More than eighty stands are set up in the historic part of town for this event.

☎ 0522828696

LANCIANO (CHIETI)

Approximately seventy stands line via Trento and via Trieste for this market.

☎ 087163640

LUGO (RAVENNA)

MERCATINO DI ARTIGIANATO
E ANTIQUARIATO
(HANDCRAFTS AND ANTIQUES)

In the loggia of the Paviglione booths offer things like fabrics, old postcards, coins, fossils, and furniture. No market in July and August.

☎ 054538453

MIRANDOLA (MODENA)

One hundred vendors show their wares in Piazza Costituente. Closed in August.

☎ 800110748 (toll free) or 053529613

MONTEGROTTO (PADOVA)

Approximately seventy stands are set up in Piazza 1 Maggio of this town known for its thermal springs, offering a delightful choice of goods and quite a few notable bargains.

☎ 049793439

MONTEROTONDO (ROMA)

L'ISOLA DEL TEMPO

(THE ISLAND OF TIME)

In this picturesque town, which is about an hour away from Rome, one hundred and fifty vendors offer a wide range of furniture and utensils that once were commonplace but now are rare.

☎ 06421381

MONZA (MILANO)

Close to one hundred vendors set up their wares along via Bergamo.

☎ 02725241

NOALE (VENEZIA)

MERCATINO DEL TROVAROBE

(FINDER'S FAIR)

This rendezvous takes place every month except April, July and August in Piazza Castello. Fifty vendors take part.

☎ 0415298711

OSTUNI (BRINDISI)

Seventy vendors set up their wares around Port San Demetrio.

☎ 0831562126

PALMI (REGGIO CALABRIA)

This market is made up of fifty vendors and it takes place in the town hall; worth seeking out chinaware and crèche figurines.

☎ 096524996

SALERNO

This market takes place on the second and the last Sunday of every month. Some sixty vendors line the quaint via dei Mercanti, offering items that come from estate sales at old country homes as well as a good deal of chinaware, not to mention various other curios.

☎ 089230411

SAN SECONDO (PARMA)

LA CASSAPANCA (THE STEAMER TRUNK)
This market takes place in the old center of town and is especially good for small antiques and rarities.

☎ 0521872696

SANT'ILARIO D'ENZA (REGGIO EMILIA)

Early modern furnishings, radios and toys are some of the items to be found on the one hundred stands that fill Piazza Repubblica.

☎ 0522451152

SERIATE (BERGAMO)

About sixty stands are set up along the arcade known as Galleria Italia.

☎ 035213185

TORINO

GRAN BALON, IL C'ERA UNA VOLTA
(ONCE UPON A TIME)
More than two hundred vendors participate in this "special edition" of the famous Balon Fair, lining via Cottelengo and Borgo Dora. The selection of objects includes high end antiques, but one can also finds interesting knick-knacks.

☎ 0114369741

VILLAFRANCA (VERONA)

About a hundred stands line Corso Vittorio Emmanuele offering almost everything imaginable, from antique furniture to collectible phone cards.

☎ 0458000065

VENZONE (UDINE)

A small market of antiques and recycled goods. There are about thirty vendors.

☎ 0432985034

The Third Saturday & Sunday of the Month

ASCOLI PICENO

Approximately one hundred and fifty vendors gather on the streets of the city center. This market specializes in crafts from the past and everything connected with the production of musical instruments.

☎ 0736253045

LUCCA

This is one of the best known and loved markets. It takes place on the streets that encircle the Duomo and boasts more than three hundred participants. Specialties of this market include furniture, objets d'art, toys, clothing, linens, oddities, bijoux and jewelry.

☎ 058391991

NAPOLI

FIERA ANTIQUARIA (ANTIQUES FAIR)

Two hundred vendors gather in the area around the Town Hall, the main location for this event, but they also spread out to surrounding areas. This fair began in 1977 and is the most important one in Southern Italy, offering an excellent selection of religious objects.

☎ 081421354

NARNI (TERNI)

Only about fifty vendors set up their wares in Piazza dei Priori, but a trip to this market is often worth it for the good deals on local artisanal crafts.

☎ 0744715362

PASSIGNANO SUL TRASIMENO (PERUGIA)

MERCATINO DEL PIDOCCHIETTO (THE LITTLE LOUSE MARKET)

This market takes place from April to October in the historic center of town; about fifty vendors take part.

☎ 075829801

RAVENNA

In the historic city center more than one hundred vendors gather to sell antiques, collectibles and rarities, as well as local handcrafted pieces.

☎ 054435404

The Third Saturday of the Month

GENOVA
In the pedestrian area known as "Quadrilatero", near via XX Settembre, more than one hundred vendors offer small antiques, collectibles, linens, old toys and prints.
☎ 010576791

OMEGNA (VERBANIA)
IL VECCHIO IN PIAZZA
(OLD THINGS IN PIAZZA)
Lining the center of town are seventy stands, displaying a wide variety of objects and knick-knacks.
☎ 0323887126

RIETI
One hundred vendors set up shop near the Duomo in Piazza Vittorio Emanuele; an entire section is devoted to artistic crafts.
☎ 07462871

VERONA

MERCATINO DELLE TRE A
(THE TRIPLE A MARKET)

Antiques, art and artisanal crafts: this market takes place in the sacristy of the basilica of San Zeno. Despite the small size of the market, a wide variety of goods are offered.

☎ 0458000065

VIGEVANO (PAVIA)

MERCATINO TRA LE COLONNE
(THE MARKET BETWEEN THE COLUMNS)

Every month, with the exception of August, about two hundred stands set up their wares in Piazza dei Martiri della Liberazione. A vast choice of objects makes this market appealing.

☎ 038222156

The Third Sunday of the Month

ANGHIARI (AREZZO)
In the historic center of this Tuscan town, close to fifty stands are arranged to offer minor antiques as well as older pieces for the home.
☎ 057523952

ARONA (NOVARA)
This market takes place on the boulevard that encircles the lake, which makes strolling through the stands particularly delightful.
☎ 0322231111

AVEZZANO (L'AQUILA)
About eighty vendors line the streets of the old section of town.
☎ 0862410808

BARI
FIERA DEL CATAPANO
About forty vendors line the basilica court. Closed in August.
☎ 0805242361

BERGAMO
Fifty vendors set up their goods in Piazza Angelici in Upper Bergamo; the special focus of this market is on graphic arts and publishing.
☎ 035213185

BORGO D'ALE (VERCELLI)

This important market, which has more than three hundred vendors, takes place near the fruit and vegetable market. A wide variety of merchandise is available, from hatpins to large pieces of furniture.

☎ 016146132

CARIMATE (COMO)

INVITO ALL'ANTIQUARIATO
(AN INVITATION TO ANTIQUES)

Approximately fifty stands are set up under the porticoes of the Torchio for this market: objects for sale include old farm machinery and country style furniture. Closed in July and August.

☎ 031792445

CITTÀ DI CASTELLO (PERUGIA)

FIERA DEL RIGATTIERE
(THE SECOND HAND VENDOR'S FAIR)

This market is made up of one hundred and fifty stands in Piazza Matteotti.

☎ 0755736458

CREMONA

Close to a hundred booths fill Piazza Stradivarius in the old part of town.

☎ 037223233

ESTE (PADOVA)

MERCATINO DELL'ANTIQUARIATO
E DEI ROBIVECCHI
(ANTIQUES AND OLD THINGS)

This market takes place in Piazza Maggiore, offering antiques, recycled goods and other curios.

☎ 0498753087

FONTANELLATO (PARMA)

This large and important market, which is made up of three hundred stands, takes place in the Piazza near the fifteenth-century Rocca di Sanvitale castle; interesting bargains abound.

☎ 0521823211

IMBERSAGO (LECCO)

This market, with one hundred and twenty vendors, is just one of the events that takes place in Piazza Garibaldi. Minor antiques, graphic arts, books and collectibles are some of the specialties. From March to November.

☎ 0399920198

MANTOVA

Piazza Castello and the area around the Ducal Palace host some sixty antique dealers each month (except July and August).

☎ 0376328253

NIZZA MONFERRATO (ASTI)

Farm tools, utensils and country-style furniture are only some of the good reasons to attend this major event in Piemonte, which draws three hundred and fifty vendors from all over Italy as well as parts of Switzerland and France. In Piazza Garibaldi.

☎ 0141530357

PADOVA

In Piazza Prato della Valle, the main square of this Venetian city, more than two hundred vendors exhibit their merchandise offering objects from the colonial period and curios from the Fifties, Sixties and Seventies.

☎ 0498753087

RECCO (GENOVA)

This is a smaller gathering than others, with only a hundred stands, but the variety is wide: small pieces of furniture, curios, phonecards, and wartime and civilian medals.

☎ 018572911

RIVOLI (TORINO)

Approximately one hundred booths gather in the historic center of town.

☎ 01195661996

ROSSANO (COSENZA)

Fifty stands enliven the center of town.

☎ 098427485

SIENA

In Piazza del Mercato approximately eighty vendors show their wares.

☎ 0577280551

SOAVE (VERONA)

Approximately one hundred tables are set up in the old part of town. Open until 6pm.

☎ 0457680648

TREVIGLIO (BERGAMO)

ANTICO IN VIA
(ANTIQUES ON THE STREET)

In the historic center of town approximately one hundred vendors display a vast selection of decorative items and curios.

☎ 03633171

TRIESTE

IL MERCATINO DELL'ANTIQUARIATO
(THE ANTIQUE MARKET)

Set up along the roads of the old part of town, this market might not have too many vendors (roughly seventy) but it offers an interesting selection of goods, especially the kinds of things you'd expect to find at a border town like Trieste, where different customs collide in unusual ways.

☎ 0406796111

VITERBO

Roughly fifty vendors set up their stalls in the neighborhood known as San Pellegrino.

☎ 07613481

The Fourth Saturday & Sunday of the Month

ANDORA (SAVONA)

MERCATINO DELL'ARTIGIANATO E ANTIQUARIATO

(THE ANTIQUE & ARTISANAL MARKET)

Roughly seventy vendors in this small country in the picturesque West-Ligurian hinterland.

☎ 019822708

MODENA

Novi Sad Park was built on the grounds where the old hippodrome once stood; the remains of the original structure host this wonderful antique market. With more than three hundred stands to visit, there is much to enjoy. Metal, in all its forms, from jewelry to agricultural tools, is one of the market highlights.

☎ 059216212

TOLENTINO (MACERATA)

Minor antiques and collectibles are the main attraction of this market, with about one hundred vendors attending.

☎ 0733972937

The Fourth Saturday of the Month

DOMODOSSOLA (MOVARA)
Near the Swiss border, the town hosts about fifty vendors: many peasant tools may be found.
☎ 0324492209

IMOLA (BOLOGNA)
Under the porticoes in the center of town, this small market—with only thirty-five vendors— exhibits a surprisingly good variety of objects.
☎ 0542642336

NOVI LIGURE (ALESSANDRIA)
In the historic center of this small city situated between Liguria and Piemonte, approximately fifty stands offer their goods.
☎ 01437721

The Fourth Sunday of the Month

ASTI
Nearly two hundred vendors gather in Piazza San Secondo for this ever-expanding market. Closed in August.
☎ 0141324554

CAMPAGNANO (ROMA)
Close to one hundred and eighty stands line via Palatina.
☎ 06421381

CHIETI
Some eighty vendors take their places along Corso Maruccino in this city of the Marches region.
☎ 087163640

MONDOVÌ (CUNEO)
MERCATO DEI PULCI (FLEA MARKET)
Seventy vendors fill Piazza Ellero in Mondovì Brei, the newer section of town.
☎ 0171693258

PIACENZA
MERCATINO DI PORTA GALERA
(PORTA GALERA MARKET)
Antique and collectibles are some of the highlights at the fifty stands that line via Roma.
☎ 0523492111

RAPALLO (GENOA)

IL TARLO (THE MOTH)

Collectibles, country-style furniture, old linens and bijoux are some of the things that make this market unique. Held in the historic center of town.

☎ 01856801

ROMA

Around one hundred and eighty vendors animate Piazza Verdi.

☎ 06421381

TORINO

FIERA DELL'USATO NELL'ANTICO BORGO REGIO PARCO (USED MARKET IN THE OLD BORGO REGIO PARK)

In Piazza Abba, and along the nearby streets, one can find collectibles, linens and more.

☎ 011748007

TREVISO

COSE D'ALTRI TEMPI (THINGS OF LONG AGO)

Around one hundred and twenty vendors line Borgo Cavour. Closed in August.

☎ 0422419195

TREZZO SULL'ADDA (MILAN)

One hundred and fifty vendors display their goods, consisting primarily of antiques and gift-ware, along the streets of the old part of town.

☎ 02725241

VEROLI (FROSINONE)

MOSTRA MERCATO DELL'ANTIQUARIATO
(MARKET - EXPO OF ANTIQUES)
This market-expo takes place every month
(except August and December) near the Duomo,
right in the center of town. Notable finds include
carved wood and fretwork, all locally made.

☎ 0775237255

The Final
Saturday & Sunday
of the Month

ANCONA
MERCATINO DELL'ANTICO
(ANTIQUE MARKET)
In Piazza del Plebiscito vendors gather to offer a wide range of collectibles and antique curios.
☎ 071201183

PERUGIA
In the Rocca Paolina, where there is an escalator that leads to the old section of town, and in the Carducci Gardens, one hundred an fifty vendors exhibit their goods.
☎ 0755736458

PIETRA LIGURE (SAVONA)
MERCATINO DELL'ANTIQUARIATO
E ARTIGIANATO
(ANTIQUE AND ARTISANAL MARKET)
This market actually begins on Saturday afternoon in Piazza XX Settembre. Fifty vendors offer a variety of antiques and creative handicrafts.
☎ 0198402321

SAN LORENZELLO (BENEVENTO)

MERCANTICO (AN ANTIQUES MARKET)

In Piazza Roma and in the old part of town, nearly forty stands show ceramic work and wrought iron, among other things. If the fifth Sunday falls in the following month, then the market is held on the fourth Sunday.

☎ 0824815263

The Final Saturday of the Month

CUNEO
IL TROVAROBE (THE COSTUME MASTER)
This market takes place in Piazza Europa and along Corso Nizza; stands offer old farming tools, used clothing and furnishings.
☎ 0171698388

COMO
In Piazza Peretta, about eighty stands offer linens, books, collectibles and various objects. No market in July and August.
☎ 0319010480

OLGIATE OLONA (VARESE)
This market is held at Villa Gonzaga and is dedicated chiefly to paper goods: books, newspapers, photographs and documents.
☎ 0331641560

SANTA MARGHERITA LIGURE (GENOVA)
Furniture from the colonial period, china, glassware and bijoux are some of the things offered by the forty stands and vendors that line the waterfront road.
☎ 010576791

The Final Sunday
of the Month

ANAGNI (FROSINONE)
Thirty vendors fill the old section of town.
☎ 07757301

CHIVASSO (TORINO)
MERCÀ D'LA TOLA (TIN MARKET)
The Tin Market and its one hundred and fifty vendors come to Piazza d'Armi in honor of the traditional iron workers. Closed in August and December.
☎ 01191151

FIORENZUOLA D'ARDA (PIACENZA)
MERCATINO DEI PULCI (FLEA MARKET)
Around sixty vendors gather in the old part of town.
☎ 05239891

FLORENCE
The second-hand goods and antiques market is open every weekday of the year and on the last Sunday of every month, except in July. Approximately one hundred vendors have stalls in the Piazza Ciompi and the variety is vast.
☎ 05523320

LECCE

One hundred tables are arranged in Piazza Libertini, near the castle, offering an exciting range of goods, including interesting chinaware and antique objects of everyday use.

☎ 0832314117

MILANO
MERCATONE DEL NAVIGLIO GRANDE (THE NAVIGLIO GRANDE MARKET)

More than two kilometers of stands (four hundred vendors) line the upper part of the Naviglio River every month except July and August. All objects are carefully chosen and quality controlled for each edition of the fair. The stores in the surrounding neighborhood remain open during the market.

☎ 02725241

PIAZZOLA SUL BRENTA (PADOVA)
MOSTRA MERCATO DELL'ANTIQUARIATO (MARKET—EXPO OF ANTIQUES)

The largest Palladian villa in the Veneto region, Villa Camerini, plays host to this extensive market of four hundred vendors, and offers a vast selection of furniture and furnishings, as well as a decent selection of military accessories.

Pro Loco Piazzola sul Brenta

☎ 0499601019

RECOARO TERME (VICENZA)

Under the porticoes of the old part of town, this market offers mainly smaller collectibles and gifts.

☎ 0444544122

SARONNO (VARESE)

About one hundred vendors come to the old section of town for this market, which specializes in artisanal work and high quality antiques.

☎ 029603011

SASSARI

L'INTROVABILE (THE UNFINDABLE)

This market-expo takes place on the via Santa Caterina, specializing in antiques, collectibles and curios, as well as local crafts and old photographic prints from the island.

☎ 079233534

Other
Important Dates

ACQUAVIVA PICENA
(ASCOLI PICENO)

Every Wednesday evening in July and August in the center of the old part of town, this market of antiques and artisan work is set up.

☎ 0735765085

ALBENGA (SAVONA)

MERCATINO DELL'ANTIQUARIATO

E ARTIGIANATO

(MARKET OF ANTIQUES AND CRAFTS)

This market takes place on Saturdays and Sundays from mid-June through August in the center of the old part of town; it is especially renowned for its china, watches, copper utensils, farming tools and creative handmade goods.

☎ 0182541351

AREZZO
FOTO ANTIQUARIA
(ANTIQUE PHOTOGRAPHS)

This market takes place in Piazza Grande on the last Sunday of April and September; it is of special interest to those who are passionate about photography, but it's appealing even to curious onlookers. The one hundred stands exhibit everything having to do with the history of photography: old cameras, lenses, wooden tripods and good used articles.

☎ 057523952

BAGNACAVALLO (RAVENNA)
LA SOFFITTA IN PIAZZA
(THE ATTIC COMES TO THE PIAZZA)

On the first Sunday of March, April and May one can find a good selection of antiques, modern pieces, artistic work and collectibles. Guided tours of the Ethnographic Center, which is dedicated to the marshland habitat and civilization, are simultaneously available.

☎ 054561312

BELLUNO
COSE DI VECCHIE CASE
(THINGS FROM OLD HOUSES)

This appealing event takes place on the fourth Sunday of the month, from June to September.

☎ 0437940083

BOLLATE (MILANO)

Every Sunday, except in August, more than three hundred vendors gather in Piazza della Resistenza.

☎ 02725241

BOLOGNA
CELÒ, CELÒ MAMANCA
This market takes place on Thursdays, in the old Jewish ghetto, behind Piazza San Martino.
☎ 051204111

CADONEGHE (PADOVA)
MERCATINO DEI PULCI (FLEA MARKET)
On the second Sunday of April, May, June, September and October some sixty vendors set up their wares in the Piazza in front of S. Andrea church, in the old part of town.
☎ 0498881911

CAGLIARI
MERCATINO DEL BASTIONE
(MARKET OF THE FORTRESS)
This market is held on Sundays in Piazza Costituzione, with about one hundred vendors displaying their wares. Local handicrafts are one of the specialties.
☎ 070668352

CATANIA
In Piazza Carlo Alberto, on Sunday mornings, approximately one hundred stalls set up shop.
☎ 800841042 (toll free)

CERVIA (RAVENNA)
MERCATINO DELL'ANTIQUARIATO,
DELL'ARTIGIANATO ARTISTICO
E DEL COLLEZIONISMO
(ANTIQUES, ARTISANAL WORK AND
COLLECTIBLES MARKET)
This market takes place on Wednesdays from 6 pm until midnight from mid-May to September.
☎ 0544993435

CESANO BOSCONE, CORSICO AND BUCCINASCO (MILANO)

MERCATINO DEI PULCI (FLEA MARKET)

More than one hundred and fifty vendors attend this triple crown of markets, which takes place every Sunday in one of three alternating towns in the Milanese hinterland. Decorative arts, nineteenth- and twentieth-century furniture and small antiques are for sale.

☎ 02725241

CEVA (CUNEO)

MERCATINO DELL'ANTIQUARIATO DI PENTECOSTE
(PENTECOSTAL ANTIQUE MARKET)

In the old center of town, more than two hundred vendors offer minor antiques.

☎ 0174721623

CEVA (CUNEO)

COSE D'ALTRI TEMPI
(THINGS OF YESTERYEAR)

This fair, which is like the one mentioned above, returns to Ceva during the week of Ferragosto (the fifteenth of August), with exactly the same number of vendors.

☎ 0174721623

CHERASCO (CUNEO)

MERCATINO REGIONALE DELLE PULCI
(REGIONAL FLEA MARKET)

On Palm Sunday, on the third Sunday of September and on the first Sunday in December, some six hundred and fifty vendors exhibit antiques, collectibles, used goods and artisanal crafts in the center of town.

☎ 0172489101

CIVITANOVA MARCHE (MACERATA)
MILIMARCHE
This market-fair takes place on a different day every September, offering collectible postcards, medals, and military publications.
☎ 0733230449

FAENZA (RAVENNA)
I MARTEDÌ D'ESTATE A FAENZA
(SUMMER TUESDAYS IN FAENZA)
On the last Tuesday in June and every Tuesday in July this antique market-expo takes place in the old center of town, accompanied by numerous events.
☎ 054625231

FERMO (ASCOLI PICENO)
MOSTRA MERCATO DELL'ANTIQUARIATO
E DELL'ARTIGIANATO (MARKET-EXPO
OF ANTIQUES AND CRAFTS)
This market comes to town on Thursdays in July and August, offering minor antiques and good deals as well as traditional local handmade objects.
☎ 0734228738

GALLIO (VICENZA)
A celebration of antiques on August 14th and 15th
☎ 0424445004

GRADARA (PESARO-URBINO)
IL PIACERE DELL'ANTICO
(ANTIQUE PLEASURES)
This antique market is held in the old part of town on Saturdays and Sundays from October to April, and on Fridays from May to September.
☎ 0541964123

GROTTAMARE (ASCOLI PICENO)

In this high medieval village on Tuesdays in July and August, antiques are the talk of the town.

☎ 07357391

JESOLO (VENEZIA)

Every Thursday in June and July this market enlivens Piazza Brescia.

☎ 0415298711

JESOLO (VENEZIA)

MOSTRA MERCATO DELL'ANTIQUARIATO (EXPO–MARKET OF ANTIQUES)

This fair, which has taken place for more than twenty years in Piazza Internazionale, is held in mid-August, around the time of Ferragosto; it lasts for three days.

☎ 0415298711

MATELICA (MACERATA)

MERCATINO DELL'ANTIQUARIATO (ANTIQUE MARKET)

This appointment takes place on Saturdays in July and August.

☎ 0733230449

MILAN

MERCATINO DELL'ANTIQUARIATO (ANTIQUE MARKET)

This market takes place on Sundays at the intersection of via Ripamonti and via Lorenzini.

☎ 02725241

MILAN

On Sundays along via Cordusio and the Galleria, approximately one hundred merchants and collectors of coins and stamps set up shop.

☎ 02725241

MILAN

This market of small antiques takes place on Saturdays along the Darsena del Naviglio Grande.

☎ 02725241

NOVENTA DI PIAVE (VENICE)

MERCATINO DELL'ANTIQUARIATO
DEL PRIMO MAGGIO
(ANTIQUE MARKET ON THE FIRST OF MAY)
Every year, on the First of May, antique stands fill the streets of this town. Objets d'art, linens and clothing are only some of the objects for sale.

☎ 0421307504

PESARO

This market is made up of seventy stands; it takes place on the third Sunday of the month, from March to October, in Piazza del Popolo.

☎ 072130462

PIEVE DI CADORE (BELLUNO)

MERCATO DELL'ANTIQUARIATO
(ANTIQUE MARKET)
This market is held in the center of town on every third weekend during the summer months, from June to September.

☎ 0376328253

PORTO RECANATI (MACERATA)

Along Corso Matteotti on Sundays in July and August, this fair offers a good selection of objects and furnishings.

☎ 0733230449

ROMANO CANAVESE (TORINO)
AL MARCÀ DI CIARAFE
(SECONDHAND MARKET)
One hundred vendors of antiques come to the center of town on the third Sunday in June.
☎ 0125713045

SALUZZO (CUNEO)
MERCATINO DI SALUZZO
(SALUZZO MARKET)
More than four hundred vendors gather in Corso Piemonte on the third Sunday in March, the last Sunday in April, the first Sunday in June, the first Sunday in July, the first Sunday in October and the fourth Sunday in November.
☎ 017543375

SAN BENEDETTO DEL TRONTO (ASCOLI PICENO)
ANTIQUA
(ANTIQUES MARKET)
Antiques and artisanal work are for sale in the center of town on the last Sundays in March.
☎ 0735592237

SAN GIORGIO CANAVESE (TORINO)
MERCÀ DLA ROBA DUVRÀ
(MARKET OF USED GOODS)
This antique market is held on the first Sunday in May.
☎ 0124450752

SARZANA

LA SPEZIA LA SOFFITTA NELLA STRADA
(ATTIC IN THE STREET)
Fifteen days in August, from 5pm to midnight
the town's historical center hosts about one hundred and fifty vendors. Clothes, jewels, furniture,
laces and carpets are just some of the possible
good deals in this market. A smaller version of
the same market takes place on Easter and every
fourth Sunday of the month.

SENIGALLIA (ANCONA)

Along via Portici Ercolani, on Wednesdays,
approximately sixty vendors show their wares.
☎ 071201183

TARANTO

MERCATO DELL'ANTIQUARIATO
(ANTIQUE MARKET)
Around eighty merchants display their merchan-
dise in the neighborhood known as Salinellai, on
Sunday mornings.
☎ 0994532383

VERRÈS (AOSTA)

In the old center of town, roughly thirty vendors
sell their wares.
☎ 0165236627

VINCI (FIRENZE)

CARABATTOLFIERA
(FAIR OF TRINKETS)
One hundred vendors show their wares on the
first of May and on the first of October in the
small town of Vittolini.
☎ 05523320

NOTES

NOTES

NOTES

NOTES

NOTES

NOTES

NOTES

NOTES

NOTES

MARINA SEVESO is a free-lance journalist who specializes in travel writing. In Europe she has been published by Mondadori, Piemme and Gallimard. She is particularly interested in local legends and customs and in visiting the town markets throughout Italy where these traditions still endure. She lives and works in Genoa.

OONAGH STRANSKY is a translator of Italian literature. Her publications include novels by Carlo Lucarelli, Giuseppe Pontiggia and Roberto Pazzi. Currently she is working on a novel by Erminia Dell'Oro. In 2000 she won an ALTA Fellow Award for her work. She lives in New York City.